How to Be a Great Leader in Early Years

of related interest

Leadership for Quality in Early Years and Playwork
Supporting your team to achieve better outcomes for children and families
Debbie Garvey and Andrea Lancaster
ISBN 978 1 90581 850 1
eISBN 978 1 90581 883 9

Health and Safety in Early Years and Childcare
Contextualising health and safety legislation
within the Early Years Foundation Stage
Bernadina Laverty and Catherine Reay
ISBN 978 1 90939 100 0
eISBN 978 1 90939 117 8

Parents, Early Years and Learning
Parents as partners in the Early Years Foundation
Stage   Principles into practice
Helen Wheeler and Joyce Connor
ISBN 978 1 90581 843 3
eISBN 978 1 90581 886 0

Spaces for Young Children
A practical guide to planning, designing and building the perfect space
Second Edition
Mark Dudek
ISBN 978 1 90796 995 9
eISBN 978 1 90796 997 3

Listening to Young Children
The Mosaic approach
Second Edition
Alison Clark and Peter Moss
ISBN 978 1 90796 926 3
eISBN 978 1 90796 942 3

Spaces to Play
More listening to young children using the Mosaic approach
Alison Clark and Peter Moss
ISBN 978 1 90478 743 3
eISBN 978 1 90796 924 9

Too Safe For Their Own Good?
Helping children learn about risk and life skills
Second Edition
Jennie Lindon
ISBN 978 1 90796 914 0
eISBN 978 1 90796 921 8

How to Be a Great Leader in Early Years

Jennie Johnson

Jessica Kingsley *Publishers*
London and Philadelphia

First published in 2015
by Jessica Kingsley Publishers
73 Collier Street
London N1 9BE, UK
and
400 Market Street, Suite 400
Philadelphia, PA 19106, USA

www.jkp.com

Library of Congress Cataloging in Publication Data
Johnson, Jennie, 1971-
How to be a great leader in early years / Jennie Johnson.
pages cm
ISBN 978-1-84905-674-8 (alk. paper)
1. Nursery schools--Administration. 2. Day care
centers--Administration. I. Title.
LB2822.7.J64 2015
372.21--dc23
2015008168

British Library Cataloguing in Publication Data
A CIP catalogue record for this book is available from the British Library

ISBN 978 1 84905 674 8
eISBN 978 1 78450 180 8

Printed and bound in Great Britain

Dedicated to my Mum, Monica Whistance,
whose untimely death meant I had to look for childcare
for my children, and as they say, the rest is history.

CONTENTS

Your Leadership Style

Your People

Your Customer

Introduction

KIDS ALLOWED is a multi-site high quality childcare group based in the North West of England. Over the years we have received many awards and accolades including outstanding grades from Ofsted and over 20 awards from both inside and outside the early years sector. We are known as both a great employer and a fabulous childcare setting.

I started Kids Allowed in May 2003 and very quickly realised that even though I am a natural leader, what mattered most to the success of the nursery was strong leadership at all levels of the organisation. To ensure colleagues got a good experience of working for Kids Allowed, and that parents and children got a 5 star service, I needed my middle and senior management to become much more skilled at being effective leaders.

I originally wrote this book to help those who had been promoted to management positions within my own organisation, but quickly realised that there was a wider audience for it. It is often the case in childcare that your best nursery nurses get the promotions, but there is a big skills gap from being a great nursery nurse and a great nursery leader.

This book has been written to help nursery owners, nursery managers, unit and room managers, seniors – all roles within the nursery that require leadership skills.

Although many settings have different names for these roles, the book is aimed at anyone who has direct reports in the early years sector.

The lessons I have learned over the years, although shared here with a bias to the early years sector, are in the main applicable to any service sector. If you manage people in a care-based service sector, there are certain to be things you will take from this book. You will quickly understand the underlying message conveyed by each chapter and it will be clear how you and your setting can benefit from them.

The book is written in a style that can be either read from start to finish, or dipped in and out of, as and when you get a spare five minutes (yes, I know that doesn't happen often in the early years sector!). The chapters have been designed for your ease of reference, so if there is a particular area of leadership that you are interested in improving right now, it will be easy to find the ideas most useful to you in the moment. I have kept the chapters short and examples to a minimum, so although different areas can overlap, you won't be faced with endless repetition and you won't be wading through pages and pages of unnecessary verbiage.

I hope you will take from this some gems that transform how you think and act in your own setting. They have certainly transformed my setting over the years, and they continue to transform it, because no setting is ever going to be perfect! So let this book support you in standing back a moment and reflecting on how to lift yourself and your team to the next level – or as we say at Kids Allowed, how to get better every day.

Your Way of Doing Things

1

Have a Primary Purpose

YOUR primary purpose should be the shared reason everyone at the nursery gets out of bed in the morning and comes to work aiming to deliver. If you ask my team what we do, they will answer 'We make children happy'.

Making children happy is our primary purpose. We keep this as a central focus of everything we do. This helps us stay true to our beliefs and to deliver fantastic childcare. It is the starting point for a shared purpose that focuses your team on the right things. If you don't have one, work with your team to come up with one. For a primary purpose to be on the tip of everybody's tongue, a jumbling sentence is not ideal. The shorter the better.

2

Have Clear Values for Your Nursery

T O ACHIEVE your primary purpose, you must define your values. Another way to think about your values is to consider your nursery's 'attitude' or sense of purpose.

If you don't already have documented values, it is best to work with your team to develop them rather than imposing them on your team without discussion. It is important that the whole team has a sense of ownership of the values, and having the team involved in creating them is the best way to achieve this.

What do you and your nursery stand for? What values do you believe in? Keep them simple and few. Too many or too lengthy and they will become difficult to remember.

If the team can't easily recall them, how are they to live and breathe them?!

Once you have established your nursery values, then your job descriptions, disciplinary procedures and the like should incorporate them. The values should be prominently displayed so that customers are aware of them and can see them as being fundamental to all you do for their children. Most importantly, your recruitment should be focused on finding great people who share those same values.

3

Have a Rhythm, Have a Way of Doing Things

WE CALL IT 'The Kids Allowed Way'. By listening, reflecting and reviewing regularly, these are the things we consider to be best practice and it's the way we do things. Consider where you can be clear about the way you do things:

- How do you conduct mealtimes?

- How do you handle activity planning?

- How to you induct new team members?

- How you settle new families?

- How do you do your transitions to school?

The more things you have a particular way of doing, the more smoothly your nursery will run. Like a well-oiled machine, it will have a good rhythm; children will know and enjoy the rhythm of the day and so will the team.

Routines are good but should not be regimented to strict times of the day. We prefer to look at a room's routine as a timeline, recognising that the exact timing may ebb and flow a little as no two days are exactly the same.

When everyone knows what they are doing, what their part is in the bigger picture and what is expected of them by your own nursery's way of doing things, the whole environment will be calmer and there will be a natural rhythm to the day. A nursery with rhythm is a much better place to work than a nursery that stumbles from one crisis to the next!

4

NOT Because We Have Always Done It That Way!

WHEN WE SET UP our nursery, we were new to childcare. We asked lots of questions, especially about why things were done in a certain way. You would be amazed how often the answer was 'because we do' or 'because we have always done it that way!' These are not answers. They probably mean the person has no real reason for doing something. If you find yourself saying this to someone, stop. Challenge yourself to give a meaningful answer. If you don't know why you are doing something, or you don't know why you are asking your team to do something, it is highly likely it is something that doesn't really need to be done.

We once had a process that we followed for around five years before someone asked 'why?' It was a mistake made in the writing of the procedure and because it wasn't challenged, or noticed, we continued doing it for no good reason. It didn't harm anyone, but it did create unnecessary work! Now one of our mantras is 'challenge the nonsense'.

5

Ensure You Are Compliant with Your Regulatory Requirements (But Dance to Your Own Tune)

I N ENGLAND, it is currently Ofsted who enforce regulatory requirements. Most countries have a regulatory body for childcare. As a minimum we must meet regulatory requirements and have robust procedures in place to protect ourselves and the children in our care.

Our sector has had to respond to numerous changes of direction by Ofsted in the last seven years. These changes are not necessarily better for the children. Although Ofsted are officially an independent body, the criteria against which they inspect and grade educators, is imposed by the government of the day. Childcare in the UK is high up on the political agenda, so the frequently changing tune that Ofsted would have us dance to is blatantly politically motivated.

I found myself saying once too often 'what will Ofsted think?' instead of 'what is right for the children?' Once I liberated myself from worrying about them, keeping 'children at the centre of all we do' was easy. We know that we already comply with all of the minimum regulatory requirements, and in fact our standards are much, much higher than the minimum standards set by the government. So, instead of allowing ourselves to be steered by whatever gimmick is currently in favour with Ofsted, we get better every day at delivering our own brand of childcare, based on our own values and beliefs. We dance to our own tune.

6

Don't Use 'Health and Safety' as an Excuse

NEVER SAY the reason for not doing something is 'health and safety.' It's a meaningless excuse. There should always be a valid explanation for why something is or is not done. For example, we put lids on hot drinks for parents, and hot drinks are not allowed in the children's rooms. We don't have this rule 'for health and safety reasons'. It is to ensure hot drinks are not spilled on the children. Use common sense and plain language. We have to come out from behind this age-old excuse and look carefully at what we do and why – or why not!

We are all concerned with the safety and well-being of children, parents, colleagues and visitors. It is when the phrase 'health and safety' is used as an excuse for no good reason that I'm riled.

Along similar lines, if you have petty rules, get rid of them. Our dress code used to state hair had to be a natural colour. Why? Will having pink hair make you a lesser childcare practitioner?

7

Take Every Opportunity to Simplify Processes and Reduce Paperwork

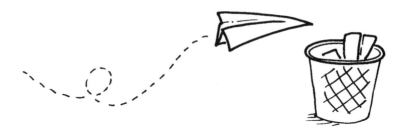

NURSERIES are awash with paperwork, often for no good reason or because a need to comply with the regulator is misunderstood. Over time, set yourself a challenge of looking with fresh eyes at every piece of paper and form you are completing and ask yourself the following:

- Why am I doing this?

- Who am I doing this for?

Often, things are being done because they always have. Another common reason is that people believe they have to do a certain task to comply with regulatory requirements. More often than not, when you look back at the actual wording of the statutory requirements, there is no need to do all this paperwork.

Any time spent completing forms and paperwork is time not spent with the children. Do your best to keep to the basics and do them to a really high standard. You will be amazed at how much unnecessary work you are doing. Observations and planning paperwork are a good place to start. I have yet to meet a nursery that is not doing too much paperwork in this area.

8

Foster a Culture of 'Getting Better Every Day'

NO MATTER how good your nursery is, there is always room for improvement. At Kids Allowed, rather than grand gestures, we focus on improving things little and often. We call this 'getting better every day.'

We get our ideas by listening. Listening to the people doing the job (the colleagues) and also listening to our customers, by way of surveys and lots of different opportunities we create for gaining valuable feedback and ideas. For example, every week I have lunch with a small group of colleagues (sandwiches and a soft drink) and I ask three simple questions:

- What can we do to make our nursery a better place to work?

- What can we do to make it better for the children and families we provide a service for?

- Do I ask you to do anything stupid? (In other words, are there policies, procedures or paperwork you do that make no sense – if so, challenge the nonsense!)

We call this initiative 'Lunch with Jennie' and without fail, great ideas for small improvements come from listening to the team over this regular informal lunch. Every team member gets an invite at least once every year and credit for ideas implemented goes back to them.

Think about how you can actively engage with your stakeholders to help you improve your service.

9

Replenish Resources Often and Keep on Top of Maintenance and Cleaning

KEEPING your nursery spotlessly clean and in impeccable condition is a must. Ongoing, high standards of maintenance is key to making this happen.

It's the same with the children's resources. Be clear about what resources each age group should have as a minimum and make sure it is always provided and in good condition.

Spending little and often to keep resources in great condition is a lot less painful than letting things slip and having to spend a small fortune to pull it back up to standard. Remember, shoddy resources and a poorly maintained nursery will lose you customers. It's a fool's economy to scrimp in this area.

It is also important for team morale to have a great working environment and the right tools to do their job. It's all part of having high standards and setting the right tone.

10

Fresh Eyes

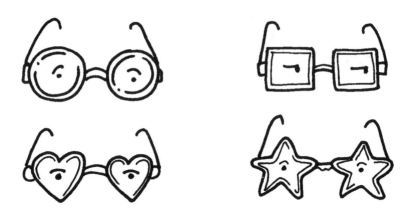

HAVING FRESH EYES is difficult. You can become blind to the obvious because you see it all day every day. This makes it an even more vital skill to learn and practise. Here are some new ways of looking that I find incredibly useful:

Make a conscious decision to regularly 'walk the customer walk'. Pull into the car park as if it's the first time. What do customers see? Is the car park a good reflection on your high standards or is it strewn with litter? Walk into the entrance, what do they see? Is it warm and welcoming? Is it clean? Does it smell fresh?

Have you ever looked at your nursery from the child's point of view? Children are tiny. Get down on their level by getting on your hand and knees and take a look at what the children see. What do they see? Are the resources accessible to them, can they see and enjoy the displays? Is it a place full of wonder that a child will want to spend the day enjoying? I am pretty sure you will make some changes when you look at your nursery through the eyes of a child.

11

Don't Tolerate Whispering in the Corner

AARGGHHH! Colleagues and customers that moan to each other instead of someone that can do something about their gripe drive me insane!

We make it clear to our colleagues that to do this is destructive, disloyal and a total waste of energy. Make sure colleagues know that it is safe to speak up about anything, and that they will be listened to. It is important that they speak to a person who can do something about their issue.

Whispering in the corner should always be challenged and in extreme circumstances should be considered a disciplinary matter – it is important that colleagues know this. We also actively encourage our parents to express their concerns through the right channels, although it is clearly not as easy to change their behaviour!

12

Speak Up

CHILDCARE is a unique sector. We are looking after children at a vulnerable age, and many have no voice of their own, simply because they are too young to communicate effectively. Speaking up for them when something is wrong is a vital part of our duty of care.

We don't just mean speaking up about abuse (which of course we must point out, if we have any suspicions at all). We must also be aware of poor childcare practice – for example, a colleague in need of more support or training. We may notice a child appearing to have learning difficulties, in need of additional support, or even unwell and in need of medical help.

All colleagues must feel they have a voice. They must feel that they can speak up without fear of recrimination. Some people think that speaking up about the behaviour of someone else amounts to 'telling tales' or 'grassing' and want to avoid getting involved. Others feel that someone else's behaviour is nothing to do with them – 'as long as I'm doing a good job, I can turn a blind eye to what another colleague is doing' or 'I don't want to get involved and be unpopular, someone else will say something.' In childcare, these views are dangerous.

From induction for new recruits, right through to regular team meetings for established colleagues, you must keep reinforcing this message. We have a simple mantra: if you don't speak up, it is as bad as is if you were doing it yourself.

13

Have a Handful of Nursery Mantras

MANTRAS stick in the psyche of a nursery. They remind everyone of what you are all about and they should link up with the primary purpose and values of your nursery. Here's a few we like to live by – you may have noticed some of them throughout the book:

- We say yes to any reasonable request.

- Follow a child's interests. Right here, right now.

- The child is at the centre of everything we do, not Ofsted!

- No whispering in the corner.

- Challenge the nonsense.

- It's easier to ask forgiveness than permission!

- If you see something wrong and don't speak up, it is just as bad as doing it yourself.

- The more you do for them, the less they learn.

What are your nursery's mantras? What do they say about your nursery and the work you do?

14

Empower Your Team to
Delight Your Customers

YOU CAN'T deliver your nursery's vision on your own. It is your team that will actually deliver your vision. Have a clear management structure. Empower and trust them to run their rooms to the high standards you have established. Ensure they know they can speak up. Encourage them to ask for help at any time and remind them that asking for your help is a strength and not a weakness.

Ensure all your colleagues know they are empowered to deliver an amazing experience to the children in your care and their families. Foster a can-do attitude. Employ motivated people who give a damn; people who have an enthusiastic sense of purpose and make things happen. You want people in your nursery who, faced with a challenge, can say 'yes' rather than people who find a million reasons why not! Encourage colleagues to use their own initiative and make the most of their own creative spirit.

Your
Leadership
Style

1

Know Your Stuff!

I F YOU ARE GOING TO LEAD in a childcare setting, you need to know your subject. In other words, you need to understand the ways children in their early years learn, the importance of this stage of development, and how to ensure their emotional well being.

Be well read. Be open-minded, but have a view. Visit the many online forums to challenge yourself and your thinking. Your childcare qualification is just the beginning of your journey – there will always be something to challenge your thinking and inspire you to reflect on how you deliver your personalised brand of childcare. Be thirsty for knowledge.

2

You Can't Know Everything

N O EXPERT in anything has all the answers. This is as true of childcare as it is of any other field – there is always more to know and more to learn. Not having all the answers can be very daunting as a nursery leader and it can be lonely too, especially when things are not going well.

There is an enormous network out there of other owners, managers and people outside the childcare sector altogether.

I can guarantee, you are not the first person to ever have had the problem you are trying to deal with. So, pick up the phone and ask someone you think can help you. You will be amazed how generous most people are with their time and support if asked in the right way.

3

Set the Tone

A N OUTSTANDING nursery manager has very high expectations of the team, the standard of care under their roof, and the overall approach to early years care and learning. Set the bar high! We are looking after precious children. Only the best is good enough.

A great leader is strong. Being a strong and effective leader always means being fair, kind and understanding, while setting and insisting upon high standards. Take a step back and be confident that your standards are achievable. Have a vision, not just of what the standard looks like, but how it can be achieved in your nursery, by your team.

Make your expectations clear and immediately challenge behaviours that do not meet your standards. Be constructive and supportive in your challenge, so that the colleague is clear on how to change in order to meet your standards and expectations. This is an essential part of fostering an empowered team.

4

Communicate

K EEP your team informed. Newsletters; an information board; inclusive team meetings; daily dashes with your management team – whatever works for you. It can be very frustrating to hear something important through the grapevine, and your team cannot be expected to make changes unless they hear about them.

Hearing from you first-hand means that they get to share your vision of where you are steering them and the nursery. In addition, you get to hear first-hand what the team think of your vision, who might be affected in ways you hadn't intended, and how you might look after the needs of your team while change is happening.

Social media is great for this purpose. For example, on Facebook you can use private groups to share information quickly and securely while also receiving valuable instant feedback. Consider setting up a private Facebook group (or similar) for your team, it is a superbly effective tool and it's free!

5

You Are Here to Serve!

I F YOU THINK being 'the boss' means lording it over your team, getting the best parking spot or no longer doing the menial jobs, you are mistaken. The higher up the nursery you climb, the more people you are there to serve.

Timpsons, the shoe repair chain (a northern-based company I deeply respect) call this 'upside down management.' This means that the people who directly serve customers are the most important people in the business – your nursery. Everybody else, including the manager and the owner are there to give support, helping the team to provide a great service to the customer.

Language, for example, can be an important sign for your team that a culture of upside down management is at work in the business. At Kids Allowed there is no 'Head Office' – instead, there is 'Central Support.' What in other workplaces might be called 'a staff meeting with the CEO' is called 'Lunch with Jennie' at Kids Allowed. We call our employees colleagues and not staff. What does your language say about how you view things?

Throughout this book, I hope you will be inspired to find ways to develop an upside-down culture in your own nursery.

6

Spend as Little Time in the Office as Possible – Even Better, Don't Have an Office

S OMETIMES managers get comfy behind a desk, hidden in an office. This is exactly the sort of manager you should not be. Leadership is about being seen. It's about being available; role-modelling; mentoring, and setting an example. All these things are impossible from behind a desk in an office. Our most successful managers are the ones that spend the least time in their office and the most time in the children's rooms.

Childcare practitioners resent managers who they rarely see. You must lead by example, model best practice, and coach and monitor your team – be a walking example of what inspirational childcare looks and feels like.

Being the nursery manager doesn't mean you no longer have to do those less glamorous things. Get stuck into the mucky jobs sometimes too! Change a nappy, mop up the gloop, sweep the sand! You shouldn't ask anyone to do something you wouldn't be happy to do yourself.

If you see litter in the car park when you arrive in the morning, don't walk over it then send someone else out to pick it up. Do it yourself, there and then. It is what you would want your team to do, isn't it? Be seen doing the little things, so your team will know it is expected of them too. It's this kind of manger that inspires others to be great, not the one that hides out in their cosy office.

7

Be Approachable and Empathetic

A N OPEN DOOR POLICY is best. You want parents and colleagues to come to you with their problems and ideas. Only have your door closed if you really need privacy, which shouldn't be often.

Be available. If somebody asks 'Do you have a minute?', do your best to stop what you are doing, give them your time and listen. Being there for people when they need you means a lot. At Kids Allowed, I give all parents and colleagues my mobile, direct dial and email address. Even with 300 plus colleagues and 1300 plus customers, this access is not abused. Make it as easy as possible for people to come to you, and when they do, listen well.

It is common to feel defensive when listening to constructive feedback. If your defensiveness comes across, this can put people off doing it again. You need that feedback – it is a vital part of improving your service. Even if on the inside you want to defend yourself and your team, it is better to listen there and then, reflect, then try to understand the other person's point of view. Perhaps even practise your poker face in the mirror!

8

If You're 'One of the Gang', It Can Make Difficult Conversations More Difficult

BEING APPROACHABLE doesn't mean you have to be everyone's best friend. You are there to lead and inspire the team. If you are also socialising with them, it can make being seen to be fair and consistent that bit harder. You must find your own balance here. For me, the team and I enjoy each other's company, but I have my own separate circle of friends outside work that I socialise with.

That doesn't mean putting a stop to the occasional team-building meal or drink. It also doesn't keep you from getting to know your team – in fact, it's really important that you do. The personal well-being of your colleagues is likely to affect how they are in work, and it may be that even small things you can help with as their manager could make a huge difference at home. Show a genuine interest in your team, their family and what makes them tick. A team member is often really touched if you ask them how their holiday was or how their child is getting on at university.

Find ways of investing some of your time in personal conversations, so that you can show a genuine interest in the personal well-being of individual colleagues, while maintaining a strictly professional relationship with them.

9

Don't Have Favourites

C LIQUES in any company are extremely destructive. Favourites are even more so. It is common to have a natural affinity with some colleagues and not with others (this is sometimes referred to as unconscious bias). This can't be helped, it is part of being human. What you can be aware of, however, is how you behave towards those you have a natural affinity with, compared with how you behave towards those you don't. You can ensure that you are not seen to have favourites.

Consistency in how you treat your team is supremely important. This is no less true in a nursery environment. If you do something for one, not doing it for another can lead to morale issues very quickly. It can cause resentment as colleagues who may be just as hard-working and committed as the next are left feeling undervalued rather than justly rewarded.

This does not mean you must treat everyone the same. Just as every child we look after is unique, so is every colleague. What works for one, may not work for another. What matters is consistency in fairness, and equal respect for every colleague. It is important to treat everyone equally, but equal does not necessarily mean the same.

10

Meaningful Praise and... Thank You!

PRAISE OFTEN and publicly. Praise much more than you criticise (criticism is usually best done in private). Give thoughtful and specific praise: 'Wow, that was a fantastic activity, the children looked totally engrossed. It was lovely to see you respond to their interests and take it further'.

This way, colleagues don't just receive praise but they also understand why they are being praised. It helps them to recognise good practice. Other colleagues will notice when someone receives glowing praise and they will reflect on how to attract admiration for their own practice too. This helps to encourage and nurture great childcare and customer service.

In addition to praise, it is important to show gratitude to your team for making your nursery what it is – for achieving those standards and meeting your expectations, perhaps even exceeding them. Make it meaningful: 'Thank you for staying behind a few minutes tonight to tidy up the home corner, it looks so much more inviting for the children tomorrow.'

Delight your team with occasional little gestures, such as cakes in the team room; birthday and thank you cards. You will be amazed at the power of the hand-written word. Not many people receive letters at home other than bills and junk, so a hand-written note from you could be a truly special and valued thing. Finally, at the very end of each day, hang around the door and say thank you to the team as they leave. Done from the heart, it really works.

11

Mistakes Happen

CHILDCARE IS A SERVICE delivered by people. People are human and will inevitably make mistakes. It is rare a person goes out of their way to intentionally do something wrong – most people wake up that morning to do a good, honest day's work. Make sure you have created an atmosphere where your team will feel they can speak up, rather than cover up a mistake for fear of the consequences. A culture of fear is not what you want.

We are clear about the difference. An honest mistake, where a person holds their hand up, is generally acceptable. There will of course be exceptions in childcare – some things are just not okay in any circumstance. However, covering up a mistake is not to be tolerated. Foster an aversion to covering up mistakes, rather than a fear of making mistakes.

An important part of fostering such a culture, is to encourage colleagues to reflect upon and learn from mistakes when they occur. If reflection and learning is shared with other colleagues and managers, then mistakes can become an important part of getting better as an individual and as a nursery.

All in all, not only do you minimise the risk of the same mistake happening again, but you add value to the professional development of the colleague, while pushing up the standards of the nursery. Recognising and sharing mistakes and difficulties is something to be encouraged.

12

Mutual Respect All Round

T HERE IS A LEVEL of respect that all colleagues can expect from each other, from you and from parents using the nursery. You are the key figure in ensuring that each colleague feels respected and supported by the company.

Occasionally, you will come across a parent that is disrespectful, a parent who thinks they can be unreasonable and shout to get their own way. Let me be clear – childcare can be highly emotive, and some concerns can be capable of bringing out the worst in a parent. A biting incident, for example, is often a trigger.

There is, however, a difference between a parent who has a one-off emotional outburst, and a parent who is routinely rude and aggressive. As the nursery leader, you must support your team – neither you, nor them should have to put up with abusive behaviour. Although it will not be an easy conversation to have, a parent who behaves like this must be made to understand that their behaviour will not be tolerated in your nursery. It must be made clear that if they want to carry on using your services, they will have to find a way to channel and express their concerns in a constructive way.

13

Look After Your Team

YOUR TEAM spend a huge portion of their waking hours at work. It is common to hear people dread Mondays and live for Fridays – how sad! Life and fun are not just for the weekends! Make sure your nursery is a fun and engaging place to work. After all, if you can't have fun in childcare, something is very wrong indeed!

At Kids Allowed you may be surprised to know we hold our colleagues' happiness at equal priority with the children's happiness. We spend just as much of our management time making sure the team are as happy as the children. We do this because we absolutely believe that we cannot deliver our primary purpose of 'making children happy' without a happy team to deliver it.

Your
People

1

Recruit Great People

C HILDCARE is unusual in that most countries have laws governing the number of adults required to look after each individual child in your care. This can make recruitment suddenly become urgent. However, the minute you start to prioritise filling roles in haste to meet ratios, ahead of finding great people, the problems start and the rot sets in. You must always recruit great people that share your values and approach.

Recruit people with the right attitude. Don't focus only upon qualifications. A lack of qualifications could be easily remedied by supporting the new recruit in gaining them. Changing a poor attitude into a great attitude is much more difficult.

If you do take on unqualified colleagues, part of their job offer should be to gain a childcare qualification within a given timeframe. In extraordinary circumstances, we make exceptions. At Kids Allowed, we have a grandmother who has three children and seven grandchildren, so she has asked to be exempt. We agreed. She could probably teach us a thing or two! We are not saying qualifications don't matter. We are only saying that they matter less than finding fantastic people with a fabulous attitude.

2

Involve Your Team in the Recruitment Process

A T KIDS ALLOWED, peer reviews are part of the recruitment process. Potential new colleagues work in the rooms for a few hours, then the existing team are asked a very simple question: 'If the candidate is successful, would you be happy having him or her working in your room?'

The responses we receive from peer reviews are by no means the only factor we consider when deciding whether or not to make a job offer, but we do take the team's reactions into account. Asking this question really gets the team thinking about what makes an ideal candidate for working in this nursery, and to take some responsibility for that too. It also allows the team to feel involved and listened to. It's an engaging way to make recruitment enjoyable and inclusive, and everyone benefits from being part of this vital process.

We also financially reward colleagues when their recommendation of a candidate results in a great new recruit. This means that they are on the lookout for potential candidates outside of the workplace. Their involvement in the recruitment process means that they are likely to recommend people who they know would be perfect for the role and great to work with.

3

Get Rid of Toxic Employees

I T ONLY TAKES ONE toxic employee to turn a happy, fun environment into something miserable and lifeless. Just one person's toxic attitude can have a devastating affect on your nursery.

Anyone can have a bad day, even a bad week. Personal problems added to everyday stresses can take their toll on even the most positive and optimistic member of the team. For these people, the team is their work family and they will look for support from colleagues and from you.

The toxic employee has negativity as a default setting. They seem almost incapable of optimism and resent the optimism of others, stamping out happy moments and draining positive energy from the life of the nursery.

Toxic employees must be rooted out and dealt with, either by turning them around into great team members (it can be done) or by showing them the door. Once you have done this, the morale of your team will be transformed. In fact, they will probably ask why it took you so long to sort it out! Dealing with toxic colleagues is one of your most important roles as a leader.

4

Duvet Days Are Not Okay

LOOK at your sickness levels. Are they high? Do you have a problem with a few colleagues who think it's okay to have Monday off because they are tired or hungover from a weekend of partying? Sickness levels are a good indication of how engaged your team are. A passionate, enthusiastic team will usually be reflected in low sickness levels.

Childcare is quite unique in that the work won't wait. An absent team member is a big problem as you need to be 'in ratio', so it is really important to have a clear and strong policy around sickness and absence. It will help you to deal with longer-term and genuine sickness and absence in a supportive way and it will also help you to effectively deal with colleagues who are taking advantage, by ensuring your policy allows you, if necessary, to consider absence a disciplinary matter when appropriate. Your role as a manager is to know the difference between the two and deal with each appropriately.

5

Professional Development

A NURSERY needs skilled and knowledgeable childcare practitioners. A deep understanding of a child's development and their needs at this very special age is vital. You can never know too much.

To support this, make sure your team have regular access to professional development. At my nursery, there are regular, mandatory training sessions and events that colleagues are contractually obliged to attend.

Training and even routine team meetings must be lively and engaging. Don't just talk at your team. You must make learning interactive and fun if you want it to be remembered. Inspire a thirst for knowledge in your team and encourage them to take a proactive interest in their own self-improvement.

First Aid training is vital. Ensure everybody has this important skill. Would every member of your team know what you do if a child started choking or convulsing? In this emergency situation, you don't want to be trying to find your first aider – even a short time delay could be the difference between life and death.

6

Find Time to Have Appraisals More Often Than Once a Year

I T SIMPLY doesn't make sense to spend quality one-to-one time with a valuable team member only once a year. Do it more often if you can and unless it is a life or death scenario, don't cancel an appraisal. It sends a very negative message to a colleague if you delay their appraisal because something else has come up. You are indirectly telling that team member they are not as important as whatever else came up.

Decide what works for you. We find doing a short appraisal every other month works for us. It's a one-to-one meeting to reflect on what's going well and to celebrate it. It's also an opportunity to discuss what could be going better and put a plan in place to implement changes. We use it to discuss any training or other professional development the team member would like to access. It doesn't have to be lengthy and doesn't have to involve reams of documentation; it's a living, breathing, action based approach that supports our 'getting better every day' culture.

A more regular appraisal also means that difficulties are identified much sooner and strengths are progressed and made the best of straight away, rather than waiting a whole year to find that a colleague would have done a fantastic job but for a short training course or an opportunity to put personal talents to good use.

7

Encourage the Team to Solve Their Own Problems

YOU DON'T NEED TO get involved in everything! For example, if a team member can't work their shift on the rota, let them swap with a colleague and inform you of the solution. By adopting this approach, you will find you have more time and thought-space for leading and managing, without getting bogged down with the minute detail of every decision made. If your policies are strong and effective, they will provide adequate guidance for the team to solve many problems without your direct supervision.

In the process, the team are gaining a deeper understanding of your way of doing things.

With a little space to be responsible and autonomous, your team can be more creative and feel proud of their decisions and the changes they help to bring about, rather than feeling stifled by over-bearing supervision and control as they blindly follow your instructions.

8

Listen to Your Team

Y OUR TEAM deliver your service day in, day out. They know the issues better than anyone. They are familiar with the challenges and the things that are going well or not so well. Your way of doing things will improve with the input of those who are actually doing the job – it seems such an obvious point! If you want to get better every day your team should be helping to shape how the nursery do things. Fostering a culture of challenge and making small improvements based on feedback will transform your service. This will help make your nursery a special place to be part of, with valued employees and customers.

Your team know what frustrates them and what gets in the way of them giving the children an amazing experience. Often, these are the very things you are asking them to do (like paperwork and form filling) which seemed like a good idea when you designed them at your desk! So encourage your team to challenge the nonsense. Ask them directly: 'Do I ask you to do anything that seems stupid?'

Find a forum to encourage your team to share ideas. For us, an example of this is 'Lunch with Jennie.' Make sure you give the team and the individuals that come up with the great ideas the credit for these ideas. Listening, sharing best practice, improving your service and recognising your team's contribution is a great habit to get into.

9

Challenge Poor Practice

CONFLICT is hard. Too many managers choose to ignore poor practice rather than challenge it. Managers who avoid conflict are simply not doing their job. It is vital that your team have clear expectations of how they are to interact with the children in your care, so you must challenge things that fall below your standards.

Sometimes it will be the little things, such as closed rather than open interactions with children. This needs a gentle touch and diligent mentoring to enhance understanding and approach.

Sometimes it's what we call 'redline stuff'. Shouting, and raised voices are examples of this – we just don't do it. In these situations a much firmer approach is needed. Remove the colleague from the situation immediately. Reflect with them on what they have done and ask what they should have done instead. Ask yourself whether this is a training issue. Are they properly informed about your expectations? Or are they just not cut out for childcare?

It is one of a manager's most important roles to act and intervene. When you let poor practice go unchallenged, or worse, let 'redline stuff' go unchallenged, you are in effect saying it is okay. You are sending the message that this behaviour meets with your expectations. This is how poor practice can creep into becoming accepted, and eventually the norm.

10

Have Transparent Pay Scales. Be as Generous as You Can Afford

C HILDCARE is a poorly paid sector. The pay in no way reflects the level of responsibility our teams take on themselves all day, every day. However, asking parents to pay more for the care we give (and we all know parents already struggle with childcare fees) is unlikely to be the answer to the problem.

However, as colleagues are promoted within the nursery, reward them as generously as you can. Although it is not possible to pay everyone what they truly deserve, you can pay your unit manager more to reflect the extra responsibility. Published pay grades allow the team to see what it is possible to achieve if they work hard.

We pay based on responsibilities rather than qualifications, so our senior nursery nurses and other senior staff earn significantly more than a 'living wage', as they deserve to. Consider what you can do to address this difficult balance. Be as generous as you can, within the boundaries of what is viable for your nursery.

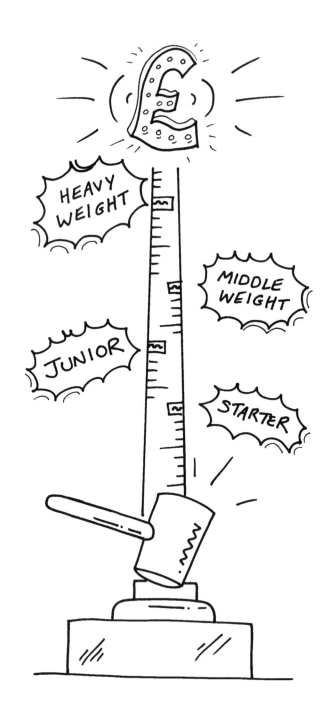

11

Recognise and Reward (Financially or Otherwise)

C OLLEAGUES should be reliable, trustworthy and there to do a great job. When these qualities are recognised in a colleague, it is important to reward them. Recognition alone can be a reward and costs nothing or next to nothing.

For example, we ask colleagues and parents to vote for parent and team heroes. The winners and runners up receive a trophy and a list of the lovely comments made about them by the voters. It is a great motivator and, when linked to the delivery of your values, or an outstanding customer experience, this is a very effective reward system. We also have cards that can be filled out by a team member or parent, thanking and praising a colleague who has gone the extra mile for them. I personally read each one, add a hand-written note and post the card to their home address.

In childcare, 100% attendance is hugely important to the smooth running of the service. At Kids Allowed, we reward 100% attendance by allowing the colleague their birthday as an extra day's holiday the following year. It means a lot and it doesn't cost the earth. Think about ways you can reward your great team members.

Every year, we have an award ceremony, a glamorous event to celebrate our very best people, including our rising stars and unsung heroes. These ceremonies are a highlight of the year and lots of people get to be recognised for their contribution. Use any excuse to say well done for exceptional performance in a memorable and public fashion.

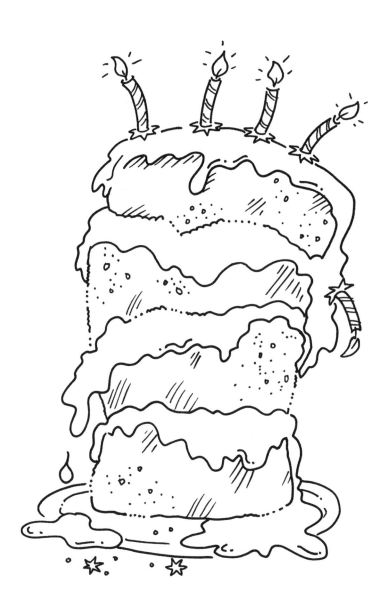

12

Long Service Awards

EVERYONE loves a familiar face and parents like to see a company with excellent retention. They especially love bringing younger siblings to the same nursery their older child attended and seeing those familiar faces. For the children too, stability and familiarity is important at the early years stage of development. Finding ways to retain your people and reward their excellence and loyalty is hugely important.

Five years' service at Kids Allowed is rewarded with a spa day for the colleague and a friend. Many take their partner or a parent along so the goodwill is spread beyond the person you are rewarding. These days, with the many last-minute discount companies like Groupon, even on a budget you can spoil your long-serving colleagues. It's your call, but I find that five years is a good benchmark and we are making big plans for how to reward 10 years' service!

13

Mark Special Moments in Your Team's Lives

REMEMBER, any excuse to do something special. When something special happens in a colleague's life, make a fuss: 21st, 40th, 50th, wedding, a new baby, graduation, anything really. These are all important opportunities to go the extra mile, showing your team you know what's going on in their life and that you care. Hand-written cards sent to home addresses work well. I have had very positive feedback from colleagues who report sharing with their families the great feeling of being valued at work.

14

A Free Brew

A FEW tea bags, coffee, milk and sugar don't cost a lot. Provide it free for colleagues and customers. They will really value it. Everyone hates a fridge awash with labelled milk!

If you can afford to take it further, consider a few extras in the team room: bread, butter, sandwich fillings and a fruit bowl. How about a four-slice toaster rather than a two-slice toaster so the team can get their food quickly? These are all small gestures that show you are thinking about your team's comfort and needs. It's easy to reinforce the message; your team are a valued resource and you want to take care of them in significant ways that you can afford.

15

Give Pay-Day Advances

MOST COMPANIES pay salaries in arrears. In a low paid sector, colleagues can sometimes get into difficulty towards the end of the month. The last thing we want is team members turning to payday lending companies and getting further into debt.

Instead, we give payday advances. Simple rules can protect your cash from being at risk of not being paid back – an example is only lending what a team member has already earned. You may be frightened everybody will ask at once, creating a cash flow problem and an administration nightmare; this is just not our experience. People only ask if they really need help, and that doesn't happen nearly as often as you might expect.

Your
Customer

1

Everyone Is a Potential Customer

R EMEMBER that everyone who comes into contact with your nursery is a potential future customer or employee.

Over the years, people who deliver the produce, provide services, pick up the post, fix the photocopier and provide our professional services have often become customers. Some have gone on to recommend friends and family to work for us.

A company that lives and breathes its values will stand out from the other companies those people visit. When they hear of someone wanting a recommendation for a nursery, they will think of you. Make sure they think of you for the right reasons!

2

Listen to Your Customers

J UST as your team 'deliver the service', your customers experience the service. They know what they like and they will have a view on what could be done better. Encourage this dialogue; customers have great ideas and feel valued when their ideas are listened to and implemented. Face to face dialogue is certainly best, and that is another good reason to be visible in the nursery as much as possible. In addition to knowing I am regularly around for a chat, on joining our nursery, every customer is given my email address and mobile phone number (now that's a brave CEO!).

As a nursery manager you are in charge of the care being given, so make sure you are very visible to your customers. Make an effort to know the children and their parents' names. Stand at the door and welcome them every morning. Do the same at the end of the day as they leave. The more accessible and visible you are, the more likely a customer will be to share their ideas and get any issues off their chest. Make it easy for your customers to talk to you.

There are many additional avenues for feedback, such as surveys and open evenings, which can be extremely useful. However, I cannot stress enough that simply being accessible and visible is essential for listening to your customers.

3

Encourage Your Customers to Complain

WHEN A NEW FAMILY joins your nursery, make sure to introduce yourself as the manager, and get to know them. Let them know you are very accessible and that you want them to raise any concerns or niggles, no matter how small. Let them know that they can do this either with the team or with you directly.

Leaving your child in the care of someone else is a very emotional event and parents can often bottle up concerns because they feel vulnerable and worry there will be consequences for them or their child if they complain. So make it really easy for them. Explain that you want them to tell you how to make your nursery better.

Stress that you want to know about everything down to the littlest things. Small niggles can soon become big frustrations if they are not nipped in the bud – before you know it you could be dealing with a very unhappy parent or colleague. Even worse than a child leaving your nursery without explanation is finding out they left due to a problem that could have been easily resolved.

Actively encourage customers to complain. As crazy as it might sound, it makes a lot of sense.

4

Learn From Every Complaint

U NHAPPY customers can become your biggest advocate if you handle their concerns properly. Don't be tempted to just offer a quick fix. Look at why the complaint has been made and be sure to fully understand the following:

- What went wrong?

- Why did it go wrong?

- What was at the root of the problem?

- What can we learn from it?

- Do we need to change anything to mitigate it happening again?

- Do we need to improve our training?

Be open with your customer. Tell them what you have found when looking into their concern. Tell them what you have learned and what you are going to do to put it right for them. Also be sure to tell them what you will do to minimise the chance of it happening again.

If you handle a complaint well, you will often turn an unhappy customer into a delighted customer and advocate of your nursery. As a result, your business, how it does things, and your customer relationships will all have improved.

5

Recognise the Importance of 'Parent Handover' at the Beginning and Especially the End of the Day

A CHILD may have spent nine wonderful, inspiring hours in your care and had an absolutely fantastic time. Be aware that the parent will not know any of this unless it is reflected in what they see and what you tell them during that five minute window at the end of the day. It is so easy to give a false impression that the care you have given their child all day is below the standard they rightly expect.

Parents get very frustrated when all they are told is 'They have been fine' – a totally meaningless update that says nothing useful. Make sure your practitioners understand how important these few minutes are and that they communicate effectively what their child has done that day; what they were most interested in; what they achieved; how they were feeling and what delighted them. It will make all the difference to the parent.

6

Have One True Place for Communication

DOES your nursery have the communication equivalent of chickenpox? We call it poster rash! Information all over the place and so much of it that the very people you are trying to communicate with start to ignore it!

Think about a place within your nursery where you can communicate all the important things. This 'one true place' can become somewhere it is easy to keep information current and remove things as they become outdated. It also means parents know where to look when they want this valuable information.

7

Take Advantage of Social Media

I T'S FREE, and a great way to communicate and engage with customers.

It's a great addition to a website and newsletters, allowing you to share ideas, do surveys, or even a quick 'hands up' question such as 'we are thinking about serving fruit rather than cake after lunch, what do you think?' It's a great way to involve customers' in shaping your policies.

It is also useful for showing parents what children in the rooms have been doing and learning about, as well as reminders about plans for activities, such as on World Book Day.

Of course, make sure you have parental consent to use pictures of children. Remember to take sensible precautions. For example, don't use children's names online and don't post about a trip before you go. Instead, post an update about it when you have returned.

8

Share Your Educational Approach with the Parents

A NURSERY must have a clear approach to childcare. For us, a big part of the message we want parents to embrace is our ethos that children learn best through play and not by being 'hot housed' or having formalised education.

Don't assume your parents know your approach. You need to share it with them and reinforce it often. The more you and your parents are on the same page, the better a child's early experiences will be. For example, as part of nursery tours for prospective parents, we are clear that children will often do messy activities. This way, there are no surprises down the line when their children come home with paint on their clothes, for example.

Run short regular workshops to encourage parents to mirror your approach when at home. Parents feel really empowered when they have a better understanding, not just of what they are doing, but why they are doing it.

9

Be Honest with Parents and Ensure Your Team Are Too

HONESTY in childcare is very important. Parents must be able to trust you. Be aware that if parents feel they are being lied to, you will lose that trust and it will be very hard to regain.

For example, if a child has seemed unhappy or lethargic today, don't tell the child's parent they had a wonderful and super-energetic time! They might prefer to hear that, but they must be told the truth about their own child. This is very important for the child's well-being too – after being told about how their child was today, the parent might then want to look out for any signs of sickness or worries that the child might have. It could be that home is a little stressful right now and your report of how their child has been could stir them to take extra care over how their little one is feeling about things. Similarly, if a child has engaged in challenging behaviour such as biting, the parent needs to know that. Be tactful, but be truthful too.

10

Listen to the Children in Your Care

AS CHILDREN get older and are able to express themselves, they often have great ideas too. Your practitioners should keep their ears open for suggestions and make sure they represent the children's ideas and requests.

The school-age children we look after are invited to be involved in creating rules for their rooms, helping them feel safe, engaged and valued. They also request resources they would like to use or trips they would like to go on. They absolutely love it when the things they have suggested actually happen.

Jennie Johnson
Chief Executive Officer and Founder
Kids Allowed

ABOUT THE AUTHOR

Jennie set up Kids Allowed following the difficulties she found sourcing high quality, flexible childcare for her own daughters. With the first centre operational in 2005, Kids Allowed now has five centres in the North West with more on the way.

Jennie also established the Kids Allowed Academy in 2013 to address the needs of better quality training and qualifications for the sector and has an active apprenticeship programme. Jennie has an infectious enthusiasm for delivering the best possible service for children and their families, while making her nursery a great place to work, and earning the company and Jennie herself numerous awards.

Jennie lives in Didsbury with her husband and three children Jessica (18) Jasmine (14) and Olivia (5).

You can follow Jennie on twitter **@KA_Jennie**

www.kidsallowed.com